LET'S-READ-AND-FIND-OUT SCIENCE®

Stage 2

A DROP OF BLOOD

BY PAUL SHOWERS · ILLUSTRATED BY EDWARD MILLER

HarperCollins*Publishers*

HarperCollins®, ≈®, and I Can Read Book® are trademarks of HarperCollins Publishers Inc.

Copyright © ...

Text copyright © ... by Paul Stewart
Illustrations copyright © 2003 by Edward Miller III
Manufactured in China by South China Printing Company Ltd. All rights reserved.

Library of Congress Cataloging-in-Publication Data

Stewart, Paul.
A ring of tricks / by Paul Stewart ; illustrated by Edward Miller.
    p.   cm. — (The magical children : Stone 2)
Summary: A simple introduction to the computation and decomposition of ...
ISBN 0-06-009108-4 — ISBN 0-06-009109-X (pbk.) — ISBN 0-06-009110-3 (lib. bdg.)
[1. Magic—Juvenile literature.] I. Miller, Edward, III, ill. II. Title.

513.2—dc21

A DROP OF BLOOD

OH, THERE'S BLOOD IN
YOUR ARMS AND LEGS,
THERE'S BLOOD IN YOUR
FINGERS AND TOES,
AND ONCE IN A WHILE WHEN
A GAME GETS TOO ROUGH,
YOU'LL FIND THAT THERE'S
BLOOD IN YOUR NOSE.

There is blood everywhere inside your body. When you cut yourself, you make a hole in your skin. Blood leaks out through the hole. If the cut is small, it soon stops bleeding.

You don't have to cut yourself—or bump yourself—
to find out where the blood is. You can see where it is.
You can look at your blood with a flashlight.
Go into the bathroom tonight and shut the door.
Turn on the flashlight in the dark. Hold your
fingers over the light. What color are they?

Look in the mirror in the dark. Hold the flashlight behind your ear. What color is your ear? Shine the flashlight in your mouth. What color are your cheeks? The blood in your fingers and your ear and your cheeks makes them look red.

Blood is red because it is full of tiny red cells that float in a watery fluid called plasma. The red cells are very tiny. There are hundreds—and thousands—and millions—of them in a single drop of blood.

Red cells are too small to see with your eye. You have to look at them under a microscope. Then the red cells look like this—round and flat, thin in the middle, thick around the edge—something like tiny doughnuts without any holes.

Red blood cells
under a microscope

9

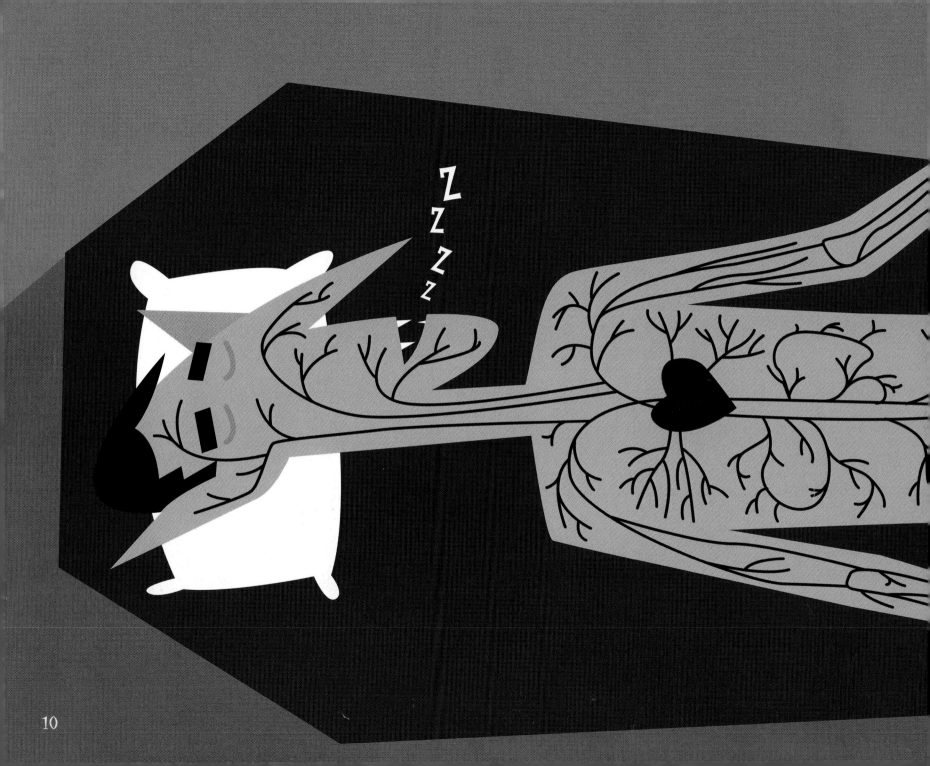

The blood is always moving inside your body. Your heart pumps it and keeps it moving. It moves through little tubes—your blood vessels. It moves out to the tips of your fingers. It moves up to your head and down to your toes.

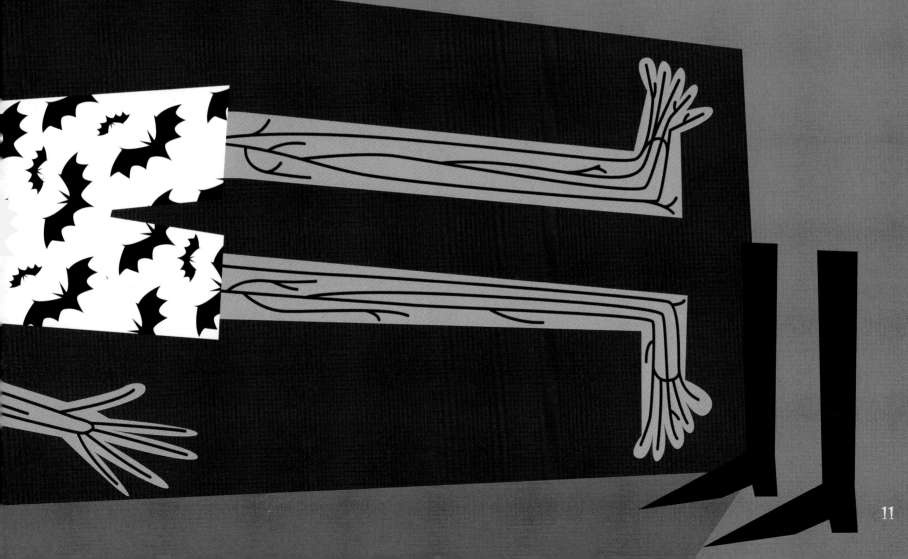

The red cells in your blood carry oxygen. Oxygen is part of the air you breathe. You cannot see oxygen, but you cannot live without it. Your body has to have oxygen every minute. You breathe oxygen into your lungs. The red cells in your blood take the oxygen from your lungs. Red cells carry the oxygen to every part of your body.

They carry oxygen to your muscles—to your bones—your brain—your stomach and intestines—your heart.

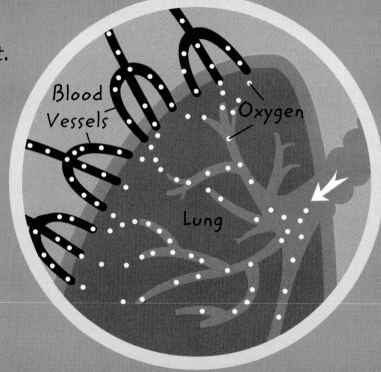

Blood Vessels

Oxygen

Lung

Cross section of the lung

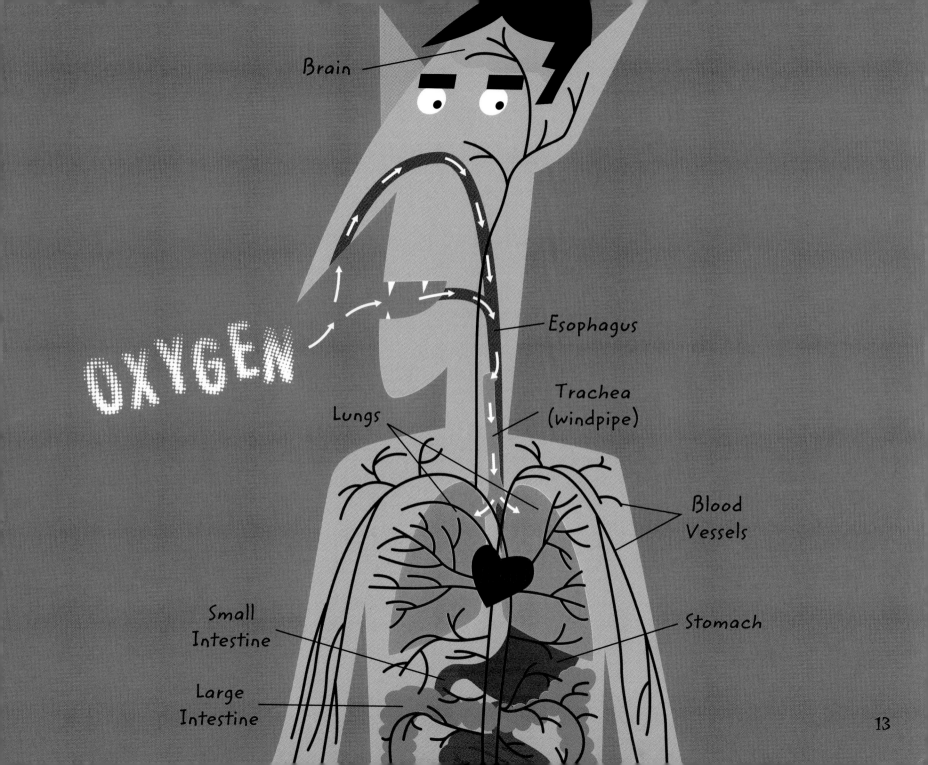

Brain

OXYGEN

Esophagus

Trachea
(windpipe)

Lungs

Blood
Vessels

Small
Intestine

Stomach

Large
Intestine

13

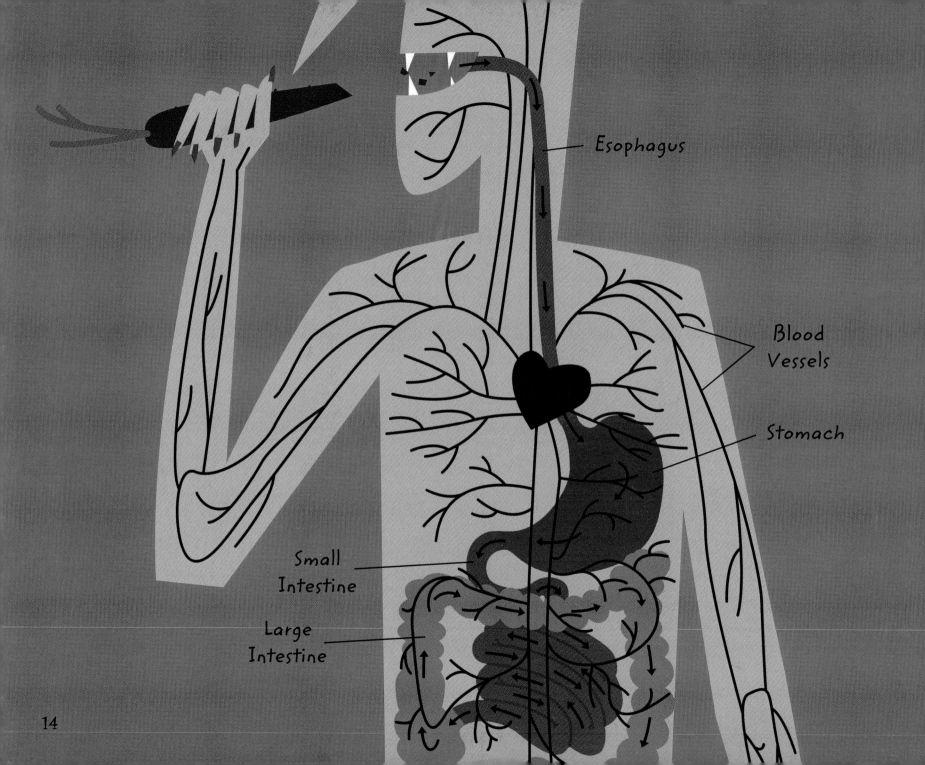

Esophagus

Blood
Vessels

Stomach

Small
Intestine

Large
Intestine

14

Your body needs food as well as oxygen.

When you eat, the food goes down to your stomach and your intestines. There food is changed into a fluid. The fluid moves from your intestines into your blood. You cannot see the food anymore, even under a microscope. But it is in your blood.

Your blood takes the food and oxygen to every part of your body. It takes food to your bones to make them grow, to your muscles to make them strong, to your fingers and your toes— even to your brain.

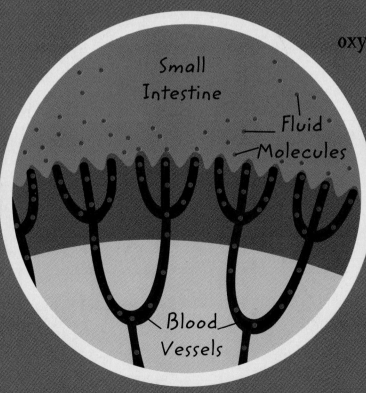

Small Intestine

Fluid Molecules

Blood Vessels

Cross section of the small intestine

White blood cells
under a microscope

There are white cells in your blood, too. They are bigger than red cells. Your blood has fewer white cells than red cells. But there are thousands of white cells in one drop of blood.

White cells protect you against disease germs. A white cell wraps itself around a germ and eats it up. Then the germ cannot harm you.

A white cell eating a germ

Germs

Some things in your blood are smaller than the white cells—even smaller than the red cells. They have no color. They are flat and round, like little plates. They are called platelets.

When you cut your skin, blood runs out. Platelets gather around the cut. They form a plug that helps stop the bleeding.

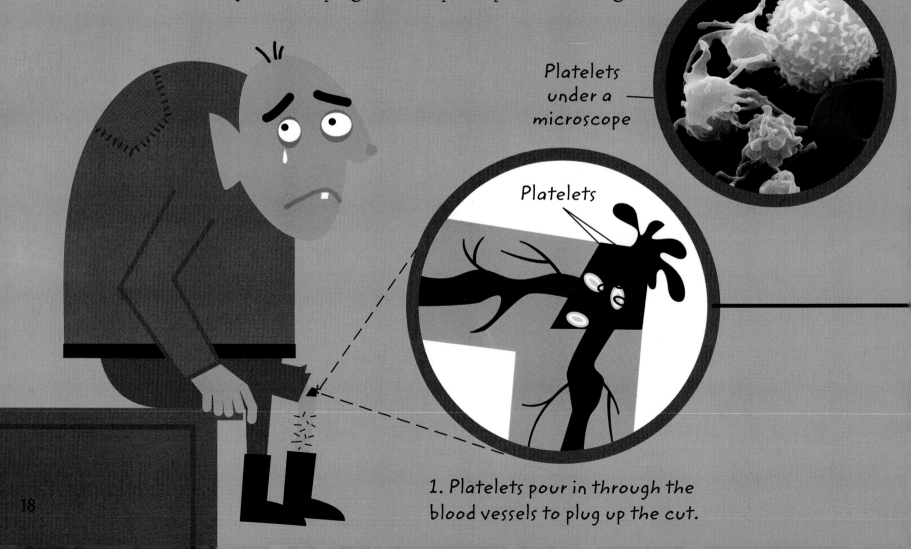

Platelets under a microscope

Platelets

1. Platelets pour in through the blood vessels to plug up the cut.

Next, the blood begins to clot. Tiny threads called fibrin form in the plasma. The fibrin threads make a net across the cut. Red cells and white cells are caught in the net. Soon the net becomes thick with red and white cells. A clot has formed. The blood cannot flow through the clot. The bleeding stops.

The clot hardens and becomes a scab. Later, new skin will grow under the scab and close the cut.

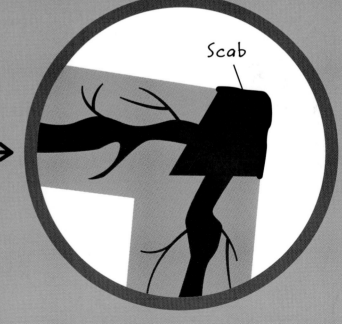

Fibrin under
a microscope

Fibrin

2. Fibrin net starts to form.

Scab

3. Scab forms.

19

Little people do not need much blood. Cathy is one year old. She weighs twenty-four pounds.

She has about one and a half pints of blood in her body. That is less than one quart.

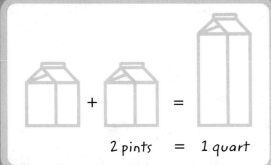

2 pints = 1 quart

Big people need more blood. Russell is eleven years old. He weighs eighty-eight pounds. He has about five and a half pints of blood in his body. That is a little less than three quarts.

An adult who is six feet tall and weighs 180 pounds has about eleven pints of blood. Eleven pints are the same as five and a half quarts.

Red cells do not last forever. They wear out. White cells and platelets wear out, too. But your body makes new red and white cells and new platelets every day.

When you cut yourself, you lose some blood. You lose red cells and white cells. You lose platelets. But that doesn't matter. Your body has plenty of new ones to take their place. It keeps making new ones all the time.

SOMETIMES I CUT MY FINGER,
SOMETIMES I SCRAPE MY KNEE,
SOMETIMES A DROP OR TWO OF BLOOD
COMES DRIPPING OUT OF ME.

THAT MEANS I LOSE SOME PLATELETS,
SOME WHITE CELLS AND SOME RED;
I LOSE THEM BY THE MILLIONS
IN EVERY DROP I SHED

BUT I DON'T GET EXCITED
ABOUT MY BLEEDING SKIN –
FOR ALL THE BLOOD THAT OOZES OUT
THERE'S PLENTY MORE THAT'S IN.

FIND OUT MORE ABOUT BLOOD

You have 100,000 kilometers of blood vessels in your body. That's long enough to circle the earth two and a half times!

Arteries carry blood that is full of oxygen and nutrients away from your heart so that your body can use them.

Capillaries connect the smallest arteries to the smallest veins.

Veins carry blood back to the heart so that the blood can be "refueled."

Your heart is a muscle, just like the muscles in your arms and legs.

The heart pumps more than 2,000 gallons of blood through the body each day.

The heart contracts 100,000 times each day.

Every year, 40,000 children are born with heart defects. Luckily, most defects can be treated with surgery or medicine.

Over 2,000 heart transplants are performed each year. When a person's heart stops working, doctors can remove the unhealthy heart and replace it with a healthy heart.

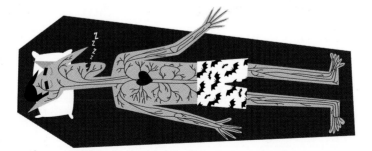

HOW TO MAKE SURE YOUR HEART STAYS HEALTHY

Don't smoke!

Eat a healthy diet. Candy, sugary soda, and salty foods can lead to heart disease when you are older. Fruits, vegetables, lean meats, and fish have the nutrients that can help you grow up to be a healthy adult.

Be active! Running, jumping, and walking, outside or in the school gym, will help your heart and body grow strong.

Have checkups regularly. Your doctor can help you learn about how your heart works and what you can do to help it stay healthy.

READ MORE ABOUT BLOOD, THE HEART, AND HOW TO BE HEALTHY AND STRONG:

FROM HEAD TO TOE by Barbara Seuling, illustrated by Edward Miller

THE HEART: *Our Circulatory System* by Seymour Simon

GOOD ENOUGH TO EAT by Lizzy Rockwell

OXYGEN

Brain

Esophagus

Trachea (windpipe)

Lungs

Blood Vessels

Small Intestine

Stomach

Large Intestine